CHOOSE THE LIVING GOD

OF

LOVE, GRACE AND GOODNESS

By

Dr David R Lumsden

God Most High

NIICOL Publishing

2020

CHOOSE THE LIVING GOD

OF

LOVE, GRACE AND GOODNESS

EPIGRAPH

"For God so loved the world, that He gave His only begotten Son, that whosoever believeth in Him, should not perish, but have everlasting life."
John 3: 16, KJV, The Holy Bible.

"Study to show thyself approved unto God, a workman that needeth not to be ashamed, rightly dividing (interpreting) the word of truth."
2 Timothy 2: 15, KJV, The Holy Bible.

Choose the Living God of love, grace, and goodness (Psalms 19) vs Satan's false, dead god(s) of destruction.

INTRODUCTION

Many people feel they can choose any god because someone they know says their god or gods will get them to an eternal place of bliss. The problem is that people are being challenged to believe in a dead god or dead gods that cannot save. How can you possibly believe that a dead god can be gracious toward you, forgive your sins, or love you with agape love (the highest and purest form of love)? If you are misled to believe in dead gods, you miss out on real life, a meaningful life worth living. Agape love and grace (favor) are characteristic of the One and Only True Living God, creator of heaven and earth and everything in the Universe. Humankind, God's crown of creation, was created to have a loving, gracious relationship of fellowship with God. Humankind was created to dwell with God for eternity in Heaven, a place of true happiness and joy.

The Fall of humankind came through Adam and Eve, because of Satan's temptation that deceived them into disbelieving and disobeying God. Satan is the source of sin and false teaching. All humankind has inherited the sinful results of the Fall. There are many teachings, worldwide, that lead people away from the true Living God of grace love, and goodness. There are not many ways, as many false teachers present, for you to be restored to a relationship of fellowship with their god. Is it not fair of God to clearly set out the Way for humankind to be restored to Him? It was not God who disobeyed, it was humankind who disobeyed God in the Garden of Eden. Is He not loving and gracious to give humankind the Way to return to Him for His favor toward eternal life, when all humanity deserves eternal punishment? You have an opportunity to receive God's favor, today, which will last you for eternity.

The Source of forgiveness, salvation (rescue from the consequences of sin: death), and the blessing of new life for now and eternity comes as a gift from the living God, through His only begotten Son, Jesus Christ. Leaders of false religions lead their people into false, dead, empty ways, which do not lead to heaven. These dead ways lead to frustration, misery, regret, and punishment for eternity in a place called hell. Why is a person sent to hell? Not all people choose to be reconciled to God through faith in the Son of God.

People need to be taught to choose the Living God for grace, and His Way of Salvation to form a new relationship (not religion) with Him that can begin immediately and last for eternity, through faith in Jesus Christ.

False teachers contradict what God says about Himself. Instead of reverencing God, they curse God or make Him out to be like a clown. Some that ridicule God, make God out to be a lesser divinity who created and rules the world. They go against His Word, which they twist and change in its intent. They deny the deity of God the Son, Jesus Christ and the deity of the Holy Spirit. They defy God's Way of salvation, to their own peril. Some say Jesus appeared to have human form only, not a true human form of body, soul, and spirit. Many argue He had a wife. Many say that He rose spiritually, but not bodily from the dead; Some religions say Jesus did not rise from the dead, but His body was stolen from the tomb. Some false teachers say that you may be saved, but you do not have the holy spirit in you. Other false teachers say you do not have the holy spirit if you do not speak in tongues. Wrong; these are non-biblical teachings. Some twist the Scriptures to justify their argument that the Bible teaches being slain in the spirit, or you can prophesy and produce extra-revelation other than God's true revelation of His truth. God says that we are not allowed to add to or take away from Holy Scripture, (Revelation 22: 7, 18-19). These False religious leaders call themselves "christian," and suggest, fraudulently, that there are other christianities. Their teachings are lies that mislead followers of their religions not to heaven, but to hell. These false spiritual leaders are not preaching the True Living God and/or they are distorting, adding to or subtracting from His Truth. Which god do they worship? These false leaders, rather, are tickling their hearers' ears. God says that we are not to be deceived by their teachings, (Matthew 24: 4; Luke 21: 8; 1 Corinthians 6: 9; Galatians 6: 7; 1 John 3: 7).

The Holy Scriptures say, God raised Jesus bodily from the dead, that He left an empty grave behind, and Jesus appeared before many witnesses, (John 20-21; Romans 8: 11). This biblical teaching is factual. False prophets, are <u>not</u> leading people into the Christianity of Jesus, the Christ, through whom you receive authentic salvation born of God (1 John 5: 1-2). These false teachers do not preach the Good News of Jesus Christ to experience the grace (love, favor and righteousness) of God. You are safe in the hands of God if you read and hide His Word in your heart and live by His Word. The God of the Holy Bible is El-Elyon, meaning God Most High (Genesis 14: 18-20; Psalms 57: 2; 78: 32-35), who loves you and wants you to receive His grace as a gift for you, without your good works. This is how you are born-again.

False prophets lead people to believe in "saints," false christs or other non-gods such as the moon god, the sun god, or the rain god, or many gods. Some give respect to a non-god using the name of God in their own language, which is only reserved for LORD GOD, the HIGHEST, the Creator. The moon god is a deception of Satan. It is not Creator GOD. Satan, the instigator behind false gods, hates rather than loves humankind. He is ready to deceive, divide, and destroy. Some false teachers teach disrespect and the destruction of memorials under the auspices of "no idols." False Teachers of non-gods are promising a happy eternity, when in fact their followers are being led into ungodly practices and therefore, to a place of punishment, regret and unhappiness, called hell. Why? They deny the deity of Jesus Christ and reject Him as their Savior and Lord as long as they live.

Only those people who accept Jesus as the Christ, their Savior and Lord, will be granted entrance into Heaven. False teachers say that Jesus is only "a god", or that He was only a "great teacher," or that He acquired special wisdom, or He was "one of many prophets," or that "He and Satan are brothers," or teach foolishly that there is no God. This is not biblical, and not God-honoring teaching. God says that the fool has said in his heart that there is no God," (Psalms 14: 1). The Holy Bible teaches that Jesus is the Son of God, the <u>Way</u> the <u>Truth</u> and the <u>Life</u>. Jesus Christ is God the Son. He was sent from God the Father to come in the flesh to save you and me, who are sinners. Those who believe God are declared righteous through faith in Jesus Christ. Jesus said unto Thomas, "I am the Way, the Truth, and the Life: no man cometh unto the Father, but by Me, (John 14: 6). Jesus means that without Jesus you cannot approach God nor enter His kingdom of heaven, (John 3: 3, 5, 7). By God the Holy Spirit you are born-again by faith placed in Jesus Christ alone. Jesus came to die so we could have <u>Life</u> through Him. God says "Believe on the Lord Jesus Christ and thou shalt be saved, you and your household," (Acts 16: 31). Whoever believes in Jesus Christ will not die the second death of eternal living punishment in hell.

All of the teachings of false prophets are Lies. These strange teachings are spread throughout the world. Some people spread the thinking that they have plenty of money, so they are okay for eternity. Some false leaders teach the prosperity gospel, which argues every person that is saved will become rich materially on this earth as a consequence. These non-biblical beliefs are lies against God's Word. Not all believers are necessarily rich in material things. All believers in Christ, saved in His name, have an eternal inheritance in Heaven; this is truth. Note, Jesus can take care of your financial needs on earth, whether you are sick or in health, and provide you with an eternal inheritance in Heaven, after you make the transition (your soul leaves your body). (Hebrews 9: 15, 27). True Christians, while on earth, rely on Jesus and learn to be content with what they are given; which is more than you will have expected for obeying God Most High. He has the best finance system going. If you lose Life by not believing on Jesus, you lose money, wealth, and the inheritance, which God promises for believers in heaven through accepting Jesus. Your end is only eternal punishment, a living death. Some think that believing in God is good enough to get to heaven; they do not need to believe in Jesus, they say. This, too, is a lie. The Holy Scriptures say, "For God so loved the world that He sent His only begotten Son; that whosoever believes in <u>Him</u> shall not perish, but have everlasting <u>Life</u>, (John 3: 16).

What happens if you do not believe in Jesus?
Earthly money and wealth do not buy God's love
for you to have eternal life. Jesus gives life for all
who repent of sin, believe in and receive Him.
Many Charismatic leaders are living high on
cheating their people and the government of
money by what they receive through donations,
while leading people down the wrong path which
leads to hell, eternal punishment. These false
teachings are running rampant throughout the
world. People who <u>do not</u> believe in Jesus, the Son
of God, perish, (John 3: 16). The Living God
explains the special judgment that he has for false
teachers: "But there were false prophets also
among the people, even as there shall be false
teachers among you, who privily shall bring in
damnable heresies, even denying the Lord that
bought them, and bring upon themselves swift
destruction,'' (2 Peter 2: 1). Their only hope is to

return to El-Elyon (the only true Living God), believe Him, repent of their sinful ways and teachings, and believe in the true God's only beloved Son, before it is too late. Don't be deceived, Jesus says. There is only One true Christianity. It was founded by the One true God, who shows you how you can become His child, assured of eternal life. He gives the promise of a home in Heaven for a true blissful eternity to every true child of God. The One true Christianity for which there is the promise of everlasting life is through faith in Jesus Christ, (John 11: 25-26). Only of His only -begotten Son does God say "This is My beloved Son in whom I am well-pleased." Only by faith in His Son does God say you can be saved. (Matthew 3: 17). For the restless soul that is agitated and anxious, Jesus says, "Come unto Me, all ye that labor and are heavy laden, and I will give you rest...learn of Me..., and ye shall find rest unto your souls..." (Matthew 11: 28-30). Take God seriously. He loves you. You can access the one true living God by coming to Him through faith in Jesus Christ, whom He sent to redeem you (pay for your sins; you do not need to work and pay off your debt of sin like a house mortgage).

Spiritual leaders in true Christianity themselves are born again and are genuine preachers of the Gospel of Jesus Christ. They interpret rightly and teach the Whole Counsel (instruction, guidance) of the God, of the Holy Bible, for true salvation. The true God (El-Elyon; God Most High) will secure you so you are travelling the right path, for the right end, eternal life. You are guaranteed a place in Heaven to live with Him forever, by His grace (favor, gift) if you trust and obey Him by following His Way, by faith in Jesus. If you reject Jesus through to your earthly death, you will be sent to hell, (Matthew 7: 22-23). It is your choice. God is not willing that you or anyone else should perish, but to come to repentance, (2 Peter 3: 9). The choice is up to you and me. You cannot change your mind in eternity. You have the freewill choice while on this earth. If you choose to go to hell for eternity, God will honor your choice, but you will regret your choice. This short booklet will take you through the ten Biblical beliefs to help you make the right choice to have eternal <u>Life</u>. God's wonderful plan of salvation and how you are secured for an eternal home in Heaven with the Creator of Heaven and earth, Himself, your creator, is what this booklet is about. God loves you and has your best interests in mind to take care of all of your needs and desires, beginning with salvation from sin's consequences, eternal living death. Appropriate (take for one's own use) the following biblical beliefs for the best interests that the Living God has for you. The choice you make at the end of this booklet will be the most

important decision you will ever make in your life.

Believe the Living God.

Are you lost, feel life is hopeless, feel lack of peace and rest in your soul, and you are afraid of death? Do you want to live like the devil and still expect to be accepted into Heaven? That will not work. You need to be born-again as Jesus said to Nicodemus in John 3: 3. Do you want to be rescued now so you have eternal life by believing God (taking Him seriously), thus trusting in His Son, Jesus Christ?

THE FOLLOWING CHOICES DETERMINE YOUR DESTINATION IN THE AFTERLIFE. WHEN APPROPRIATED (APPLIED TO YOUR LIFE), BY THE SPIRIT OF GOD, WHO IS LEADING YOU IN GOD'S WILL FOR YOU TO HAVE LIFE, FOR NOW, AND FOR ETERNITY, UPON RECEIVING CHRIST JESUS.

1: Choose El-Elyon, the living God, who exists. He exists eternally as One God in Three Persons.

The living God who loves you has approximately three hundred names. God is known by the name God, the Highest, spelled in Hebrew as El-Elyon. In Psalm 97: 9, the Psalmist says, "For you LORD

(YHWH), are Most High (El-Elyon) over all the earth, you are raised high above all the gods. This GOD, Most High is the true God the only author of true Salvation. He exists as one God-Three Persons, The Father, the Son, and the Holy Spirit, (Matthew 28: 19; 1 John 5: 7). He, only, is believed and worshipped by true Christians.

2: Choose to believe that the Word of God is true and authoritative (trustworthy) above all other written word.

All other written word must stand before God's Word as if before a Mirror to see if it is True or False. The Living God is true and trustworthy, living up to His Word.

God reveals who He is in His Holy Word. El-Elyon used another of His many names in describing Himself, as Creator.

He used Elohim. In this name, we first learn that God is one God in three Persons; God the Father, God the Son, and God the Holy Spirit. One God, all Three Persons were engaged in Creation of the Universe and everything in it, of which humankind was the crown of His creation, (Genesis 1: 1f to Genesis 3). Elohim (the same God as El-Elyon; not a different God, nor another God) took six days to create the entire universe, then He says on the seventh day He rested, which is why genuine Christians set aside one day a week for worship of God and rest only. They obey His command to keep the sabbath day holy as He says in His authoritative Word, the Holy Bible, (Exodus 20: 8). God's Holy Word, inspired by the Holy Spirit contains the instructions for how to live righteously and die peacefully. (Note, Hebrews 9: 27, "and as it is appointed unto man once to die, but after this the judgment"). By His Word, God tells you how to be saved and secured to dwell with Him in bliss for eternity. His Word also tells you about your consequences (everlasting punishment) if you reject His Way of salvation. Rather than have you perish, God wants you to believe Him and be saved.

3: Choose to believe God for the Faith which He gives to us through Christ, by His Holy Spirit.

Beliefs 1) and 2) are true, and genuine Christians believe them by faith. Hebrews 11: 1 says "Faith is the substance of things hoped for, and the evidence of things unseen." God gives you faith to be exercised in His ability to do good in your favor. Trusting God, or putting your faith in God is like you putting faith in a chair believing it will hold you when you sit down. God can be trusted even to hold the chair up underneath you're your life is a matter of faith in God. God says, "without faith it is impossible to please God," (Hebrews 11: 6). When you decide to put your faith in God for salvation, you will have made the greatest decision of your life. He will hold and protect you, never leave nor forsake you, and keep you in the palm of His hand forever. God knows those who trust Him.

4: Choose to believe God by faith about the "Fall" and what He says about the consequences of sin.

When God created humankind, the first Adam and his wife Eve, His crown of creation, He had created them good. God gave them jurisdiction over the Garden of Eden. They were to manage the Garden, but they were not to eat of the tree of good and evil. Satan, a created being turned evil because of His pride, tempted Eve and she disobeyed God by eating of the forbidden fruit. She gave some to Adam, and he sinned, too, (Genesis 3: 1-24). God made it His business to save humankind from their fall into sin. God hated their sin, but loved them, therefore, He expelled Adam and Eve from the Garden of Eden so they would not take of the tree of life and therefore, live in eternity in permanent sin and a living death, the wages of their sin. As a result of the Fall of Adam and Eve, all humanity has inherited the sin nature. God says, "For all have sinned, and come short of the glory of God," (Romans 3: 23). In Romans 6: 23a, God says "The wages of sin are death." God has a wonderful Plan of Salvation, so those of lost sinful humankind could be rescued from the second death. His Plan was that a person needed to be born again of God to have forgiveness of sins and eternal life with Him in Heaven, assured. He sent his Son Jesus Christ to come in the flesh to provide "good news" for all humankind, especially those, who would believe God. The good news of Jesus was and is that Jesus would pay the price for man's sin and buy back mankind who have been placed in sin's captivity by their own downfall, ("All have sinned and fallen short of the glory of God," Romans 3: 23). In 1 Corinthians 6: 20 God says, "For ye are bought with a price {the blood of Jesus}: therefore, glorify God in your body, and in your spirit, which are God's). God says in Romans 6: 23b, "... but the gift of God is eternal life through Jesus Christ, our Lord." God is holy, and will not allow sin into Heaven. Jesus paid the price for our redemption.

5: Choose the God who loves you and has a wonderful and amazing Plan for your Salvation, especially for all who choose to believe Him.

God is not a mean ogre waiting anxiously to punish you and throw you into hell. He hates sin, but loves the sinner.

He wants to give you a dynamic life filled with lasting meaning and purpose, John 3: 16). Mankind believes that man's main goal in life is to win or succeed in life. However, success does not mean fulness of joy in your life. God has a life with great purpose for you to find full joy, fruitfulness, and fulfillment.

Believe God for the abundance of joy He desires to give you through His Salvation in the name of Jesus Christ.

God says in His Word:

As the Psalmist says of God in Psalm 16: 11: "Thou wilt show me the path of life: in thy presence is fullness of joy; at thy right hand are pleasures for evermore."

Jeremiah 29: 11, "For I know the thoughts that I think toward you, saith the LORD, thoughts of peace, and not of evil, to give you an expected end."

John 15: 11, "These things have I spoken unto you, that My joy might remain in you, and that your joy might be full."

John 17: 13, "And now come I to thee; and those things I speak in the world, that they might have My joy fulfilled in them."

Romans 15: 13, "Now the God of hope fill you with all joy and peace in believing, that ye may abound in hope, through the power of the Holy Ghost."

Ephesians 1: 10, "That in the dispensation of the fullness of times He might gather together in one all things in Christ, both which are in heaven, and which are on earth; even in Him."

<u>6</u>: Choose the God who honors two confessions.

A) God says, "If we confess our sins, He is faithful and just to forgive us our sins, and cleanse us from all unrighteousness," (1 John 1: 9).

B) Choose to believe the Living God who sent His Son Jesus to bring the "good news" that we would not have to pay for our sins. Jesus took our place of death for our sin on the Cross of Calvary. In so doing, Jesus redeemed us about 2000 years ago. "Wherefore I give you to understand, that no man speaking by the Spirit of God calleth Jesus accursed: and that no man can say that Jesus is Lord, but by the Holy Ghost," (1 Corinthians 12: 3). God says in Philippians 2: 10-11, "that at the name of Jesus every knee should bow, of the things in heaven, and things in earth, and things under the earth; and that every tongue should confess that Jesus Christ is Lord to the glory of God the Father."

John 3: 3, "Jesus answered and said unto him (Nicodemus), Verily, verily, I say unto thee, except a man be born again, he cannot see the kingdom of God."

Best to confess Jesus as your Lord before eternity. In the afterlife, it is too late, you cannot change your mind. Now is the acceptable time, now is the day of Salvation, (2 Corinthians 6: 2). God says, "For whosoever shall call upon the name of the Lord shall be saved," (Romans 10: 13).

7: Choose to be born again by God the Holy Spirit through faith in Jesus Christ, God the Son. In Christ all things become new. Believe the Gospel (good news) of Jesus Christ. Jesus is God's Way for you to access the Highest God (El-Elyon) and to dwell with Him for eternity in Heaven.

John 3: 5, Jesus answered, Verily, verily, I say unto thee, except a man (person) be born of the water

and the Spirit, he cannot enter the kingdom of
God." Teachers repeat themselves for a good
reason, to add emphasis to a certain point of truth.
Jesus repeated Himself when talking with
Nicodemus: "You must be born-again".
When the Holy Spirit gives you new birth, you are
spiritually born-again. At the same time, the Spirit
baptizes you into Christ, i. e. into the one body of
Christ, the Church, (1 Corinthians 12: 12-14). The
Spirit of Christ gives you gifts, leads you into all
truth, and guides you in godly living for God's glory
and your enjoyment of Him. The genuine Christian
is said to be in Christ, who gives you eternal Life,
not eternal death of your soul and body. God says
it is appointed unto man once to die. For the
believer, death means the soul which has eternal
life separates from the body to be with the Lord,
(Philippians 1: 23). The soul transitions from this
life to a new world in Christ in Heaven. The soul is

reunited with the body, when Jesus comes again and raises the body unto eternal life. He will make you fit, and will usher you into Heaven. You do not need to work your way to Heaven. When you receive Jesus, you no longer need to fear death. The perfect love of God has freed you from sin and death. You do not become sinlessly perfect, but you are forgiven and given Life. Think of it; no more fear of eternal death (punishment).

God says in 2 Corinthians 5: 17, "Therefore if any man (person) be in Christ, he (she) is a new creature: old things are passed away; behold, all things are become new." You become a new person. You become a child of God, by His grace for eternity, starting from the point in time of your new birth.

8: Choose to live by the grace of the Living God in the new life, hope and joy He gives you by The Holy Spirit for victorious living.

People born again of the Spirit will have eternal life by seeing and believing in Jesus Christ. Believers will be granted the right to life in Heaven. Are "you" lost, without Jesus? Jesus said that you must be born again to be on the right path to Heaven. If not, you will not see heaven.

John 3: 7, "Marvel not that I said unto thee, Ye must be born again."

You must be born again. You are born of the Spirit when you receive Jesus Christ into your heart. That is how you become a child of God. In Christ, you are on the right path to Heaven. In Christ by faith, your soul will never face condemnation and the second death, which is eternal. Your body will be raised and united with your soul to live eternally in a new heaven and a new earth without sin, (John 5: 24; 6: 40; 8: 51; 11: 26; Revelation 21: 1-8).

You recall that no man can say Jesus is Lord but by the Holy Spirit. Being born again is acknowledging Jesus, and confessing Jesus through the leadership of the Holy Spirit. Romans 8: 14, "For as many as are led by the Spirit of God, they are the sons (children) of God." One believes on Jesus for shedding His blood for the remission of our sins, taking our place in dying on the Cross so we do not need to work hard for our salvation or fear dying and eternal death (punishment). If we depend upon our work for salvation, our work will always come up short of God's glory, and as a result we will not be known by God in Judgment Day, and therefore, be sent to hell. Jesus died in our place that we might live. On a missionary journey, a, Philippian jailor asked Paul and Silas what he needed to do to be saved. The jailor was afraid of being put to death by the Roman rulers. Paul and Silas said, "believe on the Lord Jesus Christ, and thou shalt be saved, and thy house," (Acts 16: 31). We believe that God willed for Jesus to be bodily raised from the dead by the power of the Holy Spirit for our justification to live in heaven forever with God, (Romans4: 24-25), "But for us also, to whom it (righteousness) shall be imputed (accredited), if we believe on Him who raised up Jesus our Lord from the dead. Believing in Jesus, who was delivered for our offences, and was raised (bodily) again for our justification, is the bases for a believer being declared by the Father as fit for the kingdom of Heaven. Jesus has finished all the work required for our salvation, i.e. He has paid all required for our redemption (being bought back for God; Mediator mediating on our behalf between God and man; Hebrews 9: 15), so we don't need to work our way to Heaven. That is the "good news": Salvation is a gift of God through faith in the Lord Jesus Christ, alone. Jesus said on the Cross before He died, "It is finished," (John 19: 30), i.e. His mission for our salvation for which Jesus was sent into the world, was complete. Jesus, God the Son, had appeased God the Father on our behalf so we could be declared free to live. Think, perceive, and do not fear. Eternal life is God's gift to us through faith in Jesus Christ. Believe God for what He says, "For by grace are ye saved through faith (in Jesus), that not of yourselves it is the gift of God: not of works, lest any man should boast," (Ephesians 2: 8-9). God took care of everything required for us to be saved to live eternally in Him through faith in Christ. You are eternally redeemed by opening the door of your heart to Jesus, and receiving Jesus Christ, the Son of God as your Savior and Lord. By God's grace alone through faith alone, in Jesus the Christ alone, you are saved. This gift you receive is like receiving a gift at Christmas or on your birthday. Freely, you become a child of God, secured as His child forever, (John 14: 3) because God loves you and has prepared salvation for you just as a gift.

God sent his only begotten Son to come in the flesh to live a perfect life. Then Jesus Christ allowed His life to be sacrificed as a substitute for us so we would not need to fail at working hard to pay for our sins, but rather have eternal life given to all who believe on and receive Jesus. Jesus did all the work to redeem you.

John 3: 15-17, "That whosoever believeth in Him should not perish, but have eternal life. For God so loved the world, that He gave His only begotten Son, that whosoever believeth in Him, should not perish, but have everlasting life. For God sent not His Son into the world to condemn the world; but that the world through Him might be saved."

Matthew 10: 32, Jesus said, "Whosoever therefore shall confess Me before men, him will I confess before My Father which is in Heaven." Upon receiving Christ, you are known by God.

Luke 12: 8, "Also I say unto you, whosoever shall confess Me before men, him shall the Son of man also confess before the angels of God."

Romans 10: 9-10, "That if thou shalt confess with thy mouth the Lord Jesus, and shalt believe in thy heart that God hath raised Him from the dead, thou shalt be saved. For with the heart man believeth unto righteousness; and with the mouth confession is made unto salvation."

If you confess Jesus, Jesus will make you known to the Father. God will know you in eternity, (Matthew 7: 23-24)

1 John 2: 23, "Whosoever denieth the Son, the same hath not the Father; but he that acknowledgeth the Son hath the Father also."

1 John 4: 2, "Hereby, ye know the Spirit of God: Every spirit that confesseth that Jesus Christ is come in the flesh is of God."

1 John 5: 1-2, "Whosoever believeth that Jesus is the Christ is born of God: and every one that loveth him that begat loveth him also that is begotten of Him. By this we know that we love the children of God, when we love God, and keep His commandments."

1 John 5: 5, "Who is he that overcometh the world, but he that believeth that Jesus is the Son of God?" The new life we live is not by our self-will for our self-gain, but for the glory of God through Christ by the power of His Holy Spirit who God gives all believers at the time of salvation, (Colossians2: 10).

9: Choose to believe the Living God that He makes you complete as a child of God when you open your heart to Jesus alone by faith, receiving Him as your only Savior and Lord.

Colossians 2: 10, "And ye are made complete in Him, which is the head of all principality and power." No one, nor nothing else, required.

John 1: 12-13, "But as many as receive Him, to them gave He power to become the sons (children) of God, even to them that believe on His name. Which were born, not of the blood, nor of the will of the flesh, nor of the will of man, but of God."

Believe God that if you repent of your sin and ask Him to save you, believing in the name of Jesus, God will do it, i.e. He will declare you as an adopted child of His.

John 16: 23, "And in that day ye shall ask Me nothing. Verily, verily, I say unto you, whatsoever ye shall ask the Father in My name, He will give it you."

Romans 8: 14-16, "For as many as are led by the Spirit, they are the sons (and daughters) of God. For ye have not received the spirit of bondage again to fear; but ye have received the Spirit of adoption, whereby ye cry, Abba, Father. The Spirit itself (Himself) beareth witness with our spirit, that we are the children of God."

Romans 8: 28, "And we know that all things work together for good to them that love God, to them who are called according to His purpose."

10: Choose the Living God who hears the plea of every repentant sinner when he/she prays the Sinner's Plea desiring eternal life by faith in Jesus.

Believe God to make you a child of His when you see (perceive), open your heart to Jesus and believe on Him. Jesus comes in when you open your heart to Him, during prayer, which is talking to God, because he loves you. Anyone who claims to be religious and wants to kill you by any means is not of the Living God. Believe the loving, living God, (Revelation 3: 20). Believe God will know you as His child because you trust Him through faith in Jesus Christ, (Galatians 3: 26). He wants you to have everlasting life. The prayer of repentance is the first prayer God will hear from you. This prayer has come to be known as the Sinner's Plea. When this prayer expresses the desire of your heart i.e. you truly mean what you pray, anywhere, anytime, believing in Jesus, Jesus will come into your heart and secure you for eternal life in heaven with God.

God promises he will never lose you. John 10: 28-29, "And I give unto them eternal life, and they shall never perish, neither shall any man pluck them out of My hand. My Father, which gave them Me, is greater than all, and no man is able to pluck them out of My Father's hand." You are eternally secure in Christ.

In Psalm 132, God records a prayer on the sanctuary of His place for worship. The Psalmist, begins the chapter saying,

"Lord, remember David, and all his afflictions: how he sware unto the Lord, and vowed unto the mighty God of Jacob; Surely I will not come into the tabernacle of my house, nor go up into my bed; I will not give sleep to mine eyes, or slumber to mine eyelids, until I find out a place for the Lord, a habitation for the mighty God of Jacob," (Psalm 132: 1-5). Read the full chapter to drink in the rich value of God's words.

When you think of David, you think of him as owning great riches, owning a huge palace, affording the building of a huge temple for the worship of God, and you think of him as a great king of a nation, who begat Solomon. Jesus Christ was born of the line of David, (Matt 1: 1, 6). David prepared a place for the Lord Jesus Christ.

You may be thinking that you do not have great riches, you do not have a house that radiates great wealth. You are not the king of a nation and will never be a celebrity known as the leader of a nation. You think you could never provide a sanctuary for the Lord because of all the things that you are not.

The key to David's transformation from a sinful life to a life of righteousness and glory to God, is that David opened his heart (center of feelings; the core of one's being) to the Lord for a habitation. For you it is a matter of a decision. You choose to open (yield) your heart to Jesus. Jesus will come into your heart, clean your heart, make you a child of God, become your Lord, fellowship with you, and never leave you, nor forsake you, nor lose you.

When you have Jesus, God gives you eternal life, guaranteed. In Revelation 3: 20 God says, "Behold, I stand at the door and knock: if any man hears My (Jesus) voice, and opens the door, I will come in to him, and sup (friendly fellowship) with him, and he with Me." In 1 John 5: 11-12, God says that he who has the Son has life…."

2 Chronicles 7: 14 says, "If My people, which are called by My Name, shall humble themselves, and pray, and seek My face, and turn from their wicked ways; then I will hear from Heaven, and forgive their sin, and will heal their land."

Will you confess your sin and place your faith in Jesus? Let Him make you a child of God, a new creation so to have an eternal life with God in Heaven? Say Yes and you can begin salvation and eternal life, immediately, as His gift to you, today.

If you have already given your heart to Jesus, you can pass this booklet on to someone on whom you have compassion and would love to see have Jesus in their heart for eternal life. If you have never opened your heart to Jesus, you can pray along the lines of the prayer below to open your heart to Jesus.

*You can pray the following Sinner's Plea for becoming a child of God to have a blissful (makes you happy) home for eternity, prepared for you by Jesus, (John 14: 1-6): God says, "For whosoever shall call upon the name of the Lord shall be saved," (Romans 10: 13). Believe on Jesus. He is the only one to meet your need to be born-again. Jesus, God the Son, is The Father's Way for you to be given forgiveness of sins and to become a child of God fit to live in Heaven. Read through the prayer and if it expresses the desire of your heart, then you can use it to guide you as you talk to God.

Dear Heavenly Father;

All praise to Your name; Thy kingdom of Heaven come. I'm not good enough to dwell in your great Heavenly Kingdom because of my sins. I am sorry for my sinful disobedience and rebellion against You. I confess and forsake my sins. I ask you to please forgive me of my sins. I agree with You that You sent Jesus Christ, your only begotten Son, to come in the flesh to save me. He came to pay the price for my sins so I could be bought back from sinful captivity and death, so I could live under Your grace. I do not have to work or be rich to become a child of Yours to live with You in Heaven. I believe in Jesus, who says that if I believe in Him, I will never die (the second death). I believe Your Word (John 11: 26) by faith in Jesus. I believe in Jesus as the Christ, (1 John 5: 1). I open my heart (the center of my being) and receive Jesus Christ as my Savior and Lord. Thank you, for Your forgiveness of my sins, and for giving me to Jesus for salvation. Thank you, Jesus, for coming into my heart to make my heart your habitation (dwelling place forever). Father in Heaven, thank You that you have made me complete in Jesus; that through faith in Jesus I am on the right path to Heaven, and safely in Jesus. Thank you that I have been born-again. Thank you, that through Jesus, I have access to You as my Heavenly Father. I am thankful that You have sent God the Holy Spirit into my heart to help and lead me in Your righteousness for godly living. I want to love and serve You for the rest of my life, for Your glory. Praise You. I look forward to living with you in Heaven. Believing in the name of the Lord Jesus Christ, thank you. Amen.

SIGNATURE PAGE FOR YOURSELF

If you have been serious with God, and have prayed this genuine prayer from your heart, then you have been born-again of the Holy Spirit through faith in Jesus, (Galatians 3: 26). You can sign below to help you remember the date and time you received Jesus Christ as your Savior and Lord, and you began eternal life immediately.

____

Sign Your Name

____

Date and Time

Congratulations!

Share your faith in Jesus with someone. Share about your recent decision to receive Jesus Christ as the Living God's Way and gift for you to become a child of God, to have a relationship with Him so you are secured to live with Him in Heaven forever. For confessing Jesus before humankind, Jesus will make you known to His Father and before the angels of God in Heaven. You are accepted by God and will be known by Him in Judgment Day; therefore, you will be received into Heaven though your faith in Jesus. Give thanks to God, bless, glorify, and enjoy your God, El-Elyon, which is your Father in Heaven whom you have chosen to believe. You have a personal, peaceful relationship with the Living God (Romans 5: 1). As a Christian you are no longer under the law of sin and death, but under grace (God's favor), (Romans 6: 14; Titus 3: 5-7). The Christian life is not easy, but God promises you the victory by believing in Jesus,

(John 4: 4). God holds you in His Hand, and keeps

you by His Spirit, who will raise you to live with El-

Elyon forever.

FOLLOWUP

Step 1: Read your Bible daily to receive God's instruction for you to grow spiritually. Read Matthew 11: 28 – 30. Read through the Gospel of John, and the Epistle of 1 John for a start.

Step 2: "Study to show thyself approved unto God, a workman that needeth not to be ashamed, rightly dividing the word of truth, (2 Timothy 2: 15).

Step 3: Pray daily with thanksgiving and praise to God letting your requests be known to Him in your new relationship to your Heavenly Father. The way to rejoicing is to "pray without ceasing," (1 Thessalonians 5:17).

Step 4: Find a good Bible-believing Church where the whole counsel of God's Word is being preached truthfully and faithfully. Hebrews 10: 25a says, "Not forsaking the assembling of ourselves together."

Step 5: Talk with your Bible believing and preaching pastor about:

A) Water baptism- where you are giving a public testimony of your personal salvation.

B) Communion-remembrance of what Jesus has done for you.

C) Church membership and God's blessings for you surrounding Tithing.

D) Loving and Worshipping God through serving Him and fellow members of the Church.

Step 6: Develop a Bible-based conservative evangelical theology for your Christian Life. Books that may help you get started are *ABBA'S OWN*, published and displayed on Amazon, or *ESSENTIAL CHRISTIAN THEOLOGY soon to be published.*

ABBA'S OWN has an extensive literature review and bibliographical base to assist you. You may contact the author at the email address given at the end of this booklet.

Step 7: You can say with the Psalmist, "The Lord is my rock, and my fortress, and my deliverer; my God, my strength, in whom I will trust; my buckler, and the horn of my salvation, and my high tower," (Psalms 18: 2). You will want to trust, obey, and give thanks to God daily.

Step 8: When things happen to go wrong, don't blame God and turn your back on Him, He does not cause evil. Start to praise Him more. You need His love and grace more then.

Step 9: Parents and Grandparents train up your children in the way they should go, and when they are older, they shall not depart from it, (Proverbs 22: 6). What the Living God commands us, thou shalt teach them unto our children and grandchildren, when you sit down in thy house, and when you walk by your way, and when you lie down to sleep. Your Bible needs to be an open book read in your house daily, (Deuteronomy 6: 7-8).

Father's provoke not your children to anger, lest they be discouraged, (Ephesians 6:4; Colossians 3: 21).

Step 10: God says, Husbands love your wives, and wives reverence your husbands, (Ephesians 5: 25, 33; 1 Peter 3: 7).

Step 11: Remember God's priority two commandments 1) Love the Lord your God with all your being, and 2) Love your neighbor as yourself, (Matthew 22: 37-39; Mark 12: 31; Luke 11: 27; John 13: 34).

In His Word God gives instructions for godly relationships: with Himself, with your spouses, your family, and your neighbors. Build your relationships.

Step 12: Thank God that He gave you to His Son, Jesus Christ. Thank God you were born-again by His Holy Spirit. When you opened your heart to Jesus, He came into be your Savior, Master, Lord, Coming King and God. As your Friend, He sups with you and you with Him. The person who has Christ has victory and eternal life, (1 John 5: 12). In all things give thanks to the Living God of Love, Grace and Goodness.

SUMMARY OF WHY TO BELIEVE THE LIVING GOD

55

*<u>Believe the Living God, El-Elyon, for His gift of righteousness: without which you are NOT able to see Heaven.</u>

Romans 4: 3, 23-25 "For what saith the Scripture? Abraham believed God, and it was counted unto him for righteousness," (vs. 3).

"Now it was not written for his sake alone, that it was imputed unto him; but for us also, to whom it shall be imputed, if we believe on Him that raised up Jesus our Lord from the dead; who was delivered for our offenses, and was raised again for our justification," (vs. 23-25).

Through believing on Jesus, you are pardoned from hell through faith in His death on the Cross. You have God's forgiveness for your sins through faith in Jesus' shed blood. Through faith in the resurrection of Jesus bodily from the dead for your justification, you have God's promise. You are now secured by your faith in Jesus by God's grace for your eternal home in heaven.

When you believe God in His promise of Salvation to you, when you receive and believe on Jesus Christ His Only begotten Son, He will declare you a righteous child of God welcome as his adopted child and Friend fitted through Jesus for Heaven. Guaranteed, you will never face condemnation and the second death by believing in Jesus Christ. Love the Living Triune God and serve Him with all your heart for His glory. He says that all things work out for good to them that love Him, (Romans 8: 28). He, alone, is the Living God of Love, Grace and Goodness, your choice. He is your Refuge and much more in tumultuous times through Christ Jesus.

All Scripture passages have been taken from the Holy Bible, King James Version, 1971

Other books by Dr David R Lumsden

ESSENTIAL CHRISTIAN THEOLOGY (soon, eBook and paperback)

CHOOSE LIFE (paperback)

BELIEVE GOD FOR YOU TO BECOME A CHILD OF GOD (paperback)

CHOOSE THE LIVING GOD OF LOVE, GRACE AND GOODNESS (eBook and paperback)

MARVIN SEES THE LIGHT IN A DARK WORLD (eBook and paperback)

THE STRAIT GATE TO ENTER HEAVEN (eBook)

THE HOLY SPIRIT'S MINISTRY OF INDWELLING (soon, eBook and paperback)

THE TRUE FAITH (eBook)

ABBA'S OWN (eBook, paperback, and Hardcover)

THE GOSPEL OF JESUS (forthcoming, eBook, and paperback)

THE APOCALYPTIC STORM (forthcoming, eBook and paperback)

Your copy is available or soon to be available on Amazon.com bookstore drdavidrlumsden@gmail.com

Type "Child of God" in the Subject area of your

email

Newborn International Investment Company Limited (NIICOL)

NIICOL Publishing

ΛP

2020